AMANPREET KAUR

Mastering the Interview

A Comprehensive Guide to Preparation, Performance, and Persistence

Inkwell Press

First published by Inkwell Press 2024

Copyright © 2024 by Amanpreet Kaur

All rights reserved. No part of this publication may be reproduced, stored or transmitted in any form or by any means, electronic, mechanical, photocopying, recording, scanning, or otherwise without written permission from the publisher. It is illegal to copy this book, post it to a website, or distribute it by any other means without permission.

First edition

Contents

1	Introduction	1
2	Why Preparation is Crucial	8
3	Self-Assessment	20
4	Researching the Company	28
5	Understanding the Role	36
6	Preparing Your Elevator Pitch	41
7	Common Interview Questions	48
8	Behavioral Interview Questions	54
9	Mock Interviews	61
10	Dress and Body Language	66
11	Interview Day	73
12	Follow-Up	81
13	Dealing with Rejection	87

1

Introduction

Interview preparation is a crucial step in the job search process that can significantly impact the outcome of an interview. Understanding the importance of interview preparation can help candidates effectively showcase their skills and experiences, stand out from other applicants, and increase their chances of securing their desired job or internship. In this discussion, we will delve deeply into the significance of interview preparation, exploring its benefits, key components, and best practices through examples and insights.

Importance of Interview Preparation:

Interview preparation plays a vital role in ensuring that candidates present themselves in the best possible light during the interview process. Adequate preparation helps individuals gain confidence, demonstrate their qualifications, and effectively communicate their suitability for the role. Below are some key reasons why interview preparation is essential:

1. Showcasing Skills and Experiences:
   - Example:
   - Understand the job requirements and match your skills and experiences to the role.
   - Prepare specific examples and anecdotes that highlight your achievements and contributions.
   - Practice discussing your experiences in a clear and concise manner to showcase your qualifications effectively.

2. Demonstrating Interest and Commitment:
   - Example:
   - Research the company, its culture, values, and industry to demonstrate your genuine interest in the organization.
   - Prepare thoughtful questions to ask the interviewer about the company, role, and future opportunities.
   - Showcasing your knowledge of the company can convey your commitment and enthusiasm for the position.

3. Building Confidence:
   - Example:
   - Rehearse common interview questions and responses to build confidence and reduce anxiety.
   - Practice non-verbal communication, such as posture, eye contact, and hand gestures, to appear more confident during the interview.
   - Confidence can help you present yourself positively and leave a lasting impression on the interviewer.

4. Stand Out from Other Candidates:
   - Example:
   - Tailor your responses to align with the job description and

highlight your unique selling points.
- Share specific examples of how your skills and experiences have directly contributed to solving problems or achieving results.
- Differentiating yourself from other candidates can make you a more memorable and compelling choice for the position.

5. Preparing for Different Interview Formats:
   - Example:
- Familiarize yourself with various types of interviews, such as behavioral, situational, or case interviews.
- Practice responding to different interview formats to adapt to different questioning styles and scenarios.
- Being prepared for different interview formats can help you navigate the interview process more effectively.

6. Handling Challenging Questions:
   - Example:
- Anticipate challenging questions or potential areas of concern based on your resume or experience.
- Prepare honest and thoughtful responses to address any gaps or inconsistencies in your background.
- Handling challenging questions confidently and transparently can demonstrate your ability to overcome obstacles.

Components of Interview Preparation:

Effective interview preparation involves several key components that candidates should focus on to maximize their chances of success. Some essential components of interview preparation include:

1. Researching the Company:
   - Example:
   - Explore the company's website, social media profiles, recent news articles, and industry reports to understand its background, products/services, culture, and values.
   - Identify key stakeholders, recent projects, and market trends that may impact the organization's operations.
   - Researching the company can help you tailor your responses and questions to align with its goals and priorities.

2. Understanding the Role:
   - Example:
   - Review the job description, required qualifications, and responsibilities to gain a clear understanding of the role's expectations.
   - Identify key skills, experiences, and attributes that the employer is seeking in a candidate.
   - Understanding the role can help you customize your responses to demonstrate your fit for the position.

3. Preparing Responses to Common Questions:
   - Example:
   - Compile a list of common interview questions related to your background, skills, strengths, weaknesses, and career goals.
   - Develop structured and concise responses to these questions based on your experiences and accomplishments.
   - Preparing responses to common questions can help you articulate your thoughts more effectively during the interview.

4. Practicing Mock Interviews:
   - Example:

- Conduct mock interviews with a friend, family member, or mentor to simulate real interview scenarios.
- Practice answering questions, receiving feedback on your responses, and refining your communication and presentation skills.
- Mock interviews can help you feel more prepared and confident when facing actual interviews.

5. Preparing Questions for the Interviewer:
   - Example:
   - Create a list of insightful questions to ask the interviewer about the company, team dynamics, growth opportunities, and expectations for the role.
   - Tailor your questions to demonstrate your interest in the position and gather valuable information about the company.
   - Asking thoughtful questions can showcase your curiosity, engagement, and strategic thinking abilities.

Best Practices for Interview Preparation:

To optimize your interview preparation and boost your chances of success, consider incorporating the following best practices into your routine:

1. Start Early:
   - Example:
   - Begin your interview preparation well in advance of the scheduled interview date to allow ample time for research and practice.
   - Avoid last-minute cramming and instead create a structured timeline to cover all relevant aspects of interview preparation.

2. Utilize Online Resources:
   - Example:
   - Take advantage of online resources such as company websites, Glassdoor reviews, LinkedIn profiles, and industry publications to gather information about the employer.
   - Online resources can provide valuable insights into the company's culture, interview process, and employee experiences.

3. Seek Feedback:
   - Example:
   - Request feedback on your resume, cover letter, and interview responses from peers, mentors, or career advisors.
   - Incorporate constructive feedback to refine your communication style, address potential weaknesses, and enhance your overall presentation.

4. Stay Updated:
   - Example:
   - Stay informed about industry trends, recent developments, and emerging technologies that may be relevant to the position you are interviewing for.
   - Demonstrating up-to-date knowledge can showcase your interest in continuous learning and professional growth.

5. Practice Active Listening:
   - Example:
   - Practice active listening skills during mock interviews, informational interviews, or networking events to enhance your communication skills.
   - Focus on understanding the interviewer's questions, feedback, and cues to respond thoughtfully and engage in meaning-

ful conversations.

6. Stay Positive and Confident:
   - Example:
   - Maintain a positive attitude throughout the interview preparation process and approach each practice session or research task with enthusiasm.
   - Cultivate self-confidence by visualizing successful interview scenarios, practicing positive self-talk, and acknowledging your strengths and achievements.

In conclusion, interview preparation is a critical step in the job search process that requires dedication, strategic planning, and continuous improvement. By understanding the importance of interview preparation, candidates can position themselves as top contenders for job opportunities, build confidence, showcase their skills and experiences effectively, and ultimately secure their desired roles. Through comprehensive research, tailored responses, and diligent practice, individuals can maximize their chances of success in interviews and advance their careers. Investing time and effort in interview preparation is a worthwhile endeavor that can yield long-term benefits in the form of career advancement, professional growth, and personal fulfillment.

2

Why Preparation is Crucial

Preparation is crucial for job interviews because it significantly impacts the success of the interviewee. Adequate preparation gives candidates the confidence to perform well, articulate their experiences effectively, and demonstrate their qualifications to the interviewers. By preparing thoroughly, candidates can anticipate and answer questions thoughtfully, showcase their skills and expertise, and stand out from other applicants.

Moreover, preparation helps candidates familiarize themselves with the company, its culture, and the job role they are applying for. This knowledge allows candidates to tailor their responses to align with the company's values and goals, making them more appealing to potential employers. Additionally, preparation enables candidates to ask insightful questions during the interview, showing their interest in the position and the company.

In contrast, lack of preparation can lead to missed opportunities, lower confidence levels, and poor interview performance. Candidates who do not prepare adequately may struggle to answer questions effectively, appear disinterested in the job, or fail to demonstrate their qualifications adequately. As a result, they may not make a positive impression on the interviewers and could potentially lose out on the job opportunity.

Overall, preparation plays a crucial role in interview success by helping candidates present themselves in the best possible light, showcasing their skills and qualifications effectively, and demonstrating their fit for the job and the company.

Now, let's explore the impact of preparation on interview success in more detail, examining why it is essential and how it can benefit candidates in different aspects of the interview process.

Impact of Preparation on Interview Success

Effective preparation is key to interview success as it enables candidates to approach the interview with confidence, present themselves in a positive light, and demonstrate their qualifications and skills effectively. By investing time and effort in preparing for an interview, candidates can significantly increase their chances of impressing the interviewers and standing out among other applicants. Let's explore some of the ways in which preparation influences interview success:

1. Confidence Boost

One of the primary benefits of thorough preparation is the boost in confidence it provides to candidates. When candidates are well-prepared, they feel more confident in their abilities, knowledge, and qualifications, which translates into better performance during the interview. Confidence is a key factor that can help candidates articulate their experiences, communicate effectively with the interviewers, and handle challenging questions with ease.

Example:

Sarah has an upcoming interview for a marketing position at a top firm. She spends time researching the company, reviewing common interview questions, and preparing her answers in advance. As a result, she feels confident and well-prepared when she walks into the interview room. Her confidence shines through during the interview, allowing her to convey her skills and experiences effectively and make a positive impression on the interviewers.

2. Effective Communication

Preparation plays a vital role in enhancing candidates' communication skills during an interview. By preparing responses to common interview questions, practicing their answers, and structuring their thoughts in advance, candidates can communicate their qualifications and experiences clearly and concisely. Effective communication is essential in conveying relevant information to the interviewers and showcasing how well-suited candidates are for the job.

Example:

James is interviewing for a software development position and has prepared detailed examples of his past projects and achievements. During the interview, he effectively communicates his technical skills, problem-solving abilities, and project management experience using clear and concise language. His preparation allows him to showcase his strengths in a way that resonates with the interviewers.

3. Showcasing Skills and Qualifications

Preparation enables candidates to showcase their skills and qualifications effectively during the interview. By understanding the job requirements, aligning their experiences with the role, and highlighting their key achievements, candidates can demonstrate their suitability for the position. Effective preparation helps candidates present a compelling case for why they are the best candidate for the job and why the company should hire them.

Example:

Maria is applying for a sales manager position and has researched the company's sales strategies and goals. During the interview, she leverages her past sales experience, leadership skills, and track record of exceeding targets to showcase her qualifications for the role. Her preparation allows her to paint a clear picture of how her skills align with the job requirements and how she can contribute to the company's success.

4. Tailoring Responses to the Company

Preparation involves researching the company, its values, culture, and goals, which allows candidates to tailor their responses to align with the organization's objectives. By demonstrating an understanding of the company's mission, vision, and values, candidates can show their genuine interest in the company and their motivation to contribute to its success. Tailoring responses to the company can help candidates establish a strong connection with the interviewers and differentiate themselves from other applicants.

Example:

John has an interview with a tech startup known for its innovative products and collaborative work culture. He researches the company's recent projects, reads about its values and team dynamics, and prepares examples of how his skills and work ethic align with the company's culture. During the interview, John seamlessly integrates his knowledge of the company into his responses, demonstrating his enthusiasm for the role and his alignment with the company's values.

5. Handling Challenging Questions

Preparation equips candidates with the tools and strategies to handle challenging questions during the interview effectively. By anticipating potential questions, practicing responses, and reflecting on past experiences, candidates can tackle difficult inquiries with confidence and poise. Adequate preparation helps candidates stay composed under pressure, address challenging topics thoughtfully, and provide relevant examples to support their answers.

Example:

Emma is interviewing for a project management role and knows that the interviewers may ask about a time when she faced a project setback and how she resolved it. She prepares a detailed example of a challenging project she managed, including the issues that arose, the actions she took to address them, and the outcomes achieved. When asked about a project setback during the interview, Emma confidently shares her experience, highlighting her problem-solving skills and adaptability.

6. Asking Informed Questions

Preparation enables candidates to ask thoughtful and insightful questions during the interview, demonstrating their interest in the role and the company. By researching the company, its industry, and the specific job role, candidates can generate relevant questions that showcase their curiosity, enthusiasm, and critical thinking skills. Asking informed questions not only helps candidates understand the company better but also allows them to engage in meaningful conversations with the interviewers.

Example:

David has an interview with a global consulting firm and prepares a list of questions about the company's international projects, its client base, and the challenges faced in the industry. During the interview, David asks informed questions about the firm's expansion strategy, its approach to cross-border projects, and the skills required to succeed in the consulting field. His insightful questions demonstrate his research efforts and his genuine interest in the company.

7. Demonstrating Professionalism

Preparation plays a crucial role in demonstrating professionalism during the interview. Candidates who are well-prepared exhibit a high level of professionalism by arriving on time, dressing appropriately, maintaining good eye contact, and engaging respectfully with the interviewers. Professionalism creates a positive impression on the interviewers and reflects candidates' commitment to the interview process and their desire to excel in the role.

Example:

Mark is interviewing for a customer service position and ensures he is well-prepared for the interview by researching the company, practicing his responses, and dressing in professional attire. During the interview, Mark exudes professionalism through his courteous demeanor, confident communication style, and attentive listening skills. His preparedness and professionalism leave a lasting impression on the interviewers.

In summary, preparation is crucial for interview success as it enhances candidates' confidence, communication skills, ability to showcase their qualifications, and overall performance during the interview. By investing time and effort in thorough preparation, candidates can position themselves as strong contenders for the job, make a positive impression on the interviewers, and increase their chances of securing the job offer.

Next, let's debunk some common myths about interviews that can mislead candidates and hinder their preparation efforts.

Common Myths About Interviews

Interviews can be intimidating for many candidates, and there are several common myths and misconceptions surrounding the interview process that can impact how candidates approach their preparation. By debunking these myths and setting the record straight, candidates can better understand what to expect during interviews and take proactive steps to enhance their interview performance. Let's explore some of the most prevalent myths about interviews and why they are inaccurate:

Myth 1: Interviewers Only Care About Technical Skills

One common myth about interviews is that interviewers only focus on candidates' technical skills and qualifications when making hiring decisions. While technical skills are essential for certain roles, interviewers also assess candidates based on their soft skills, cultural fit, communication abilities, and overall attitude. Employers look for well-rounded candidates who not only possess the necessary technical competencies but also demonstrate the interpersonal skills and characteristics needed to thrive in the company culture.

Debunked:

Interviewers consider a combination of technical skills and soft skills when evaluating candidates. In addition to assessing candidates' qualifications and experience, interviewers pay attention to their communication style, problem-solving abilities, teamwork skills, adaptability, and emotional intelligence. Candidates should highlight a balance of technical and soft skills during interviews to present themselves as comprehensive candidates who can contribute effectively to the organization.

Myth 2: You Should Give Perfect Answers to Every Question

Another common myth is that candidates must provide flawless, textbook answers to every interview question to impress the interviewers. While prepared responses are beneficial, overly rehearsed or robotic answers can come across as insincere and lacking authenticity. Interviewers are often more interested in understanding candidates' thought processes, decision-making abilities, and problem-solving skills rather than hearing rehearsed responses.

Debunked:

It is essential to prepare for common interview questions and practice responses to showcase one's qualifications effectively. However, candidates should focus on providing thoughtful, genuine answers that reflect their experiences and skills accurately. Interviewers appreciate authenticity and value candidates who can engage in meaningful conversations, share real-life examples, and demonstrate their suitability for the role through their responses.

Myth 3: It's All About Selling Yourself

Some candidates believe that interviews are solely about promoting themselves and highlighting their strengths, often at the expense of honesty or transparency. While it is essential to showcase one's skills and qualifications during an interview, being overly self-promotional or exaggerating one's abilities can backfire. Interviewers value authenticity, humility, and self-awareness in candidates, and appreciate honesty about both strengths and areas for development.

Debunked:

Interviews are not just about selling oneself but also about building a genuine connection with the interviewers, demonstrating a good fit with the company culture, and showing a willingness to learn and grow. Candidates should strive to present themselves authentically, communicate their achievements confidently but modestly, and express a genuine interest in the job and the organization. Being transparent about one's experiences, skills, and career goals fosters trust and credibility with the interviewers.

Myth 4: You Need to Have a Perfect Background

Some candidates mistakenly believe that they must have a flawless background, with no career gaps, mistakes, or setbacks, to succeed in interviews. In reality, interviewers understand that candidates may have faced challenges or made mistakes in the past, and they are more interested in how candidates have learned from those experiences and grown professionally. Imperfections or career hiccups do not disqualify candidates from consideration if they can demonstrate resilience, self-awareness, and a willingness to improve.

Debunked:

Having a perfect background is not a prerequisite for interview success. Interviewers are interested in hearing how candidates have overcome challenges, learned from failures, and developed professionally over time. Candidates should be prepared to address any career gaps or setbacks honestly, highlight the lessons learned from those experiences, and demonstrate their ability to adapt, grow, and add value to the organization. Showing resilience and a growth mindset can be appealing to employers.

Myth 5: The Interviewer Knows Best

Another common myth is that the interviewer holds all the power during the interview, and candidates must simply respond to the questions asked without engaging in a dialogue or asking clarifying questions. In reality, interviews are two-way conversations where candidates have the opportunity to learn more about the company, the role, and the team while also showcasing their qualifications and suitability for the job. Asking thoughtful questions and seeking clarification demonstrates candidates' interest and engagement in the interview process.

Debunked:

While interviewers play a crucial role in assessing candidates for the job, interviews are collaborative interactions where both parties engage in a dialogue to determine mutual fit.

Candidates should view interviews as opportunities to ask relevant questions, seek clarity on job expectations, learn more about the company's culture and values, and demonstrate their genuine interest in the role. Engaging in meaningful conversations with the interviewers can help candidates assess whether the company is the right fit for them as well.

By debunking these common myths about interviews, candidates can gain a more accurate understanding of the interview process and take proactive steps to prepare effectively. Understanding that interviews are holistic assessments of candidates' skills, qualifications, communication abilities, and fit with the company can help candidates approach interviews with confidence, authenticity, and a focus on building meaningful connections with the interviewers.

In conclusion, preparation is crucial for interview success as it empowers candidates to showcase their qualifications effectively, communicate their experiences confidently, and demonstrate their fit for the role and the organization. By dispelling common myths about interviews and adopting a strategic approach to preparation, candidates can position themselves as strong contenders for job opportunities and enhance their chances of securing their desired roles. Embracing thorough preparation, authenticity, and professionalism can set candidates apart in a competitive job market and lead to successful outcomes in the interview process.

3

Self-Assessment

Self-assessment is a crucial process that involves introspection and reflection to identify one's strengths and weaknesses. Understanding your skills and experiences is a key component of self-assessment, as it provides insights into areas where you excel and areas where you may need improvement. In this discussion, we will delve deeply into the concept of self-assessment, exploring its significance, methods, and examples to help individuals gain a better understanding of themselves and their capabilities.

Significance of Self-Assessment

Self-assessment plays a vital role in personal and professional development. By identifying our strengths and weaknesses, we can make informed decisions about our careers, relationships, and personal growth. Understanding our skills and experiences enables us to leverage our strengths effectively and work on improving our weaknesses. Here are some key reasons why self-assessment is important:

1. Career Development: Self-assessment helps individuals identify their strengths and interests, guiding them in choosing a career path that aligns with their skills and passions. Knowing your strengths can also help you excel in your current job or seek opportunities for career advancement.

2. Personal Growth: Reflecting on your experiences and skills allows you to recognize areas for improvement and personal growth. By acknowledging your weaknesses, you can work on them to become a better version of yourself.

3. Goal Setting: Understanding your strengths and weaknesses is essential for setting realistic goals. Self-assessment provides a clear picture of where you stand, helping you set achievable milestones and objectives.

4. Effective Communication: Knowing your strengths and weaknesses can enhance your communication skills. By understanding how you come across to others, you can adapt your communication style to convey your message more effectively.

5. Self-Confidence: Self-assessment boosts self-confidence by acknowledging your strengths and accomplishments. It helps you build a positive self-image and belief in your abilities.

6. Decision Making: Self-assessment provides valuable insights that can aid in decision-making processes. Whether it's choosing a career path, making important life choices, or solving problems, understanding your strengths and weaknesses can lead to better decisions.

Methods of Self-Assessment

There are various methods and tools that individuals can use to assess themselves effectively. Each method offers a unique perspective on skills, strengths, and areas for improvement. Here are some common methods of self-assessment:

1. SWOT Analysis: SWOT (Strengths, Weaknesses, Opportunities, Threats) analysis is a popular framework for self-assessment. It involves identifying internal strengths and weaknesses while also considering external opportunities and threats that may impact your personal or professional life.

2. Skills Inventory: Conducting a skills inventory involves listing all your skills and experiences, including technical, soft, and transferable skills. This method helps you understand the breadth and depth of your capabilities.

3. Feedback: Seeking feedback from peers, supervisors, or mentors can provide valuable insights into your strengths and weaknesses. Constructive feedback can help you gain a different perspective on your abilities and areas for improvement.

4. Personality Assessments: Personality assessments, such as the Myers-Briggs Type Indicator (MBTI) or the Big Five personality traits, can help individuals understand their personality preferences, communication styles, and work behaviors.

5. Career Assessments: Career assessments like the Strong Interest Inventory or the Holland Code can assist individuals in identifying their interests, values, and preferred work environ-

ments, helping them make informed career decisions.

6. 360-Degree Feedback: This method involves collecting feedback from multiple sources, including supervisors, peers, and subordinates, to gain a comprehensive view of your strengths and areas for development.

Examples of Self-Assessment

To provide a deeper understanding of self-assessment, let's explore some examples that illustrate how individuals can identify their strengths and weaknesses and understand their skills and experiences:

1. Example 1: SWOT Analysis

Sarah, a marketing professional, decides to conduct a SWOT analysis to evaluate her current position in the company and plan for career growth.

- Strengths: Sarah identifies her strengths as excellent communication skills, creativity in crafting marketing campaigns, and strong project management abilities.
    - Weaknesses: She acknowledges her weaknesses in digital marketing skills, public speaking, and time management.
    - Opportunities: Sarah recognizes opportunities for professional development through online courses, networking events, and cross-departmental collaborations.
    - Threats: She identifies threats such as increasing competition in the industry, limited budget for marketing initiatives, and changing consumer preferences.

By conducting a SWOT analysis, Sarah gains a comprehensive understanding of her competencies and areas where she can focus on improvement to advance her career.

2. Example 2: Skills Inventory

John, a software developer, decides to create a skills inventory to assess his technical expertise, soft skills, and professional experiences.

- Technical Skills: John lists his proficiency in programming languages such as Java, Python, and JavaScript, along with experience in web development and database management.
  - Soft Skills: He identifies his soft skills as problem-solving, teamwork, communication, and adaptability, which are essential for collaborating with cross-functional teams and handling complex projects.
  - Professional Experiences: John reflects on his past projects, highlighting successful software deployments, contributions to open-source projects, and leadership roles within his team.

Through the skills inventory, John gains clarity on his technical strengths, soft skills, and accomplishments, which can guide his career growth and future opportunities.

3. Example 3: Feedback Evaluation

Emma, a sales manager, requests feedback from her team members, peers, and supervisor to assess her leadership skills and areas for improvement.

- Positive Feedback: Emma receives positive feedback on her coaching and mentoring abilities, strategic thinking, and dedication to team success.
    - Areas for Improvement: Constructive feedback highlights areas where Emma can enhance her communication with remote team members, delegate tasks more effectively, and provide clearer performance feedback.
    - Action Plan: Emma uses the feedback to create an action plan that includes communication workshops, leadership training programs, and regular check-ins with her team to monitor progress.

By seeking feedback from multiple sources, Emma gains valuable insights into her leadership style and areas where she can grow as a manager, fostering personal and professional development.

4. Example 4: Personality Assessment

David, a recent college graduate exploring career options, takes the Myers-Briggs Type Indicator (MBTI) to understand his personality preferences and work style.

- Introversion/Extraversion: David discovers that he is an introvert who enjoys working independently and prefers quiet environments for concentration.
    - Thinking/Feeling: His results show a balanced preference for logical thinking and empathetic decision-making, indicating a blend of analytical and people-oriented tendencies.
    - Judging/Perceiving: David leans towards judging, showing a preference for structured and organized work methods over

flexibility and spontaneity.

By understanding his MBTI personality type, David gains insights into his natural inclinations, communication preferences, and potential career paths that align with his personality traits.

5. Example 5: Career Assessment

Sophia, a college student undecided about her major, takes the Strong Interest Inventory assessment to explore potential career paths based on her interests and values.

- Interests: The assessment reveals that Sophia has a strong interest in creative fields such as graphic design, writing, and digital marketing, indicating a preference for artistic and innovative work.
    - Values: She identifies values such as work-life balance, social impact, and continuous learning as essential factors in choosing a career path that aligns with her values.
    - Preferred Work Environments: Based on the assessment results, Sophia explores career options in advertising agencies, design studios, and non-profit organizations that resonate with her interests and values.

By using the Strong Interest Inventory assessment, Sophia gains clarity on potential career paths that match her interests, values, and preferred work environments, helping her make informed decisions about her academic and professional journey.

Conclusion

SELF-ASSESSMENT

Self-assessment is a reflective process that involves identifying strengths and weaknesses, understanding skills and experiences, and gaining insights into personal and professional development. By engaging in self-assessment activities such as SWOT analysis, skills inventory, feedback evaluation, personality assessments, and career assessments, individuals can gain a deeper understanding of themselves and make informed decisions about their careers, relationships, and personal growth. Through examples like conducting a SWOT analysis for career planning, creating a skills inventory for professional development, seeking feedback for leadership improvement, taking a personality assessment for career exploration, and using a career assessment for major selection, individuals can apply self-assessment tools and methods to enhance their self-awareness and leverage their strengths for success. Ultimately, self-assessment is a continuous journey of self-discovery and growth that empowers individuals to maximize their potential and pursue fulfilling paths in various aspects of life.

4

Researching the Company

Researching a company is a crucial step in many aspects of business, whether you are a job seeker preparing for an interview, an entrepreneur looking for potential partnerships, an investor considering buying stock, or a student seeking to understand the industry landscape. This process involves gathering information about a company's history, financial performance, products or services, market position, culture, and other relevant factors. By conducting thorough research on a company, individuals and organizations can make well-informed decisions that are based on facts rather than assumptions or hearsay.

In this article, we delve into the importance of company research and explore strategies for gathering information effectively. Understanding the significance of this research and knowing how to go about it can provide you with a competitive edge in various business contexts. Whether you are a seasoned professional or a novice in the business world, mastering the art of company research can open doors to new opportunities and help you navigate the complex business landscape with confidence.

The Importance of Company Research

Conducting research on a company is essential for several reasons:

1. Understanding the Company's Background: Before engaging with a company in any capacity, it is crucial to have a comprehensive understanding of its history, values, mission, and vision. By researching the company's background, you can gain insights into its origins, growth trajectory, key milestones, and overall corporate ethos. This knowledge can help you align your goals, values, and strategies with those of the company, enabling more effective collaboration and communication.

2. Assessing Financial Health: One of the primary reasons for researching a company is to evaluate its financial health and performance. By examining financial statements, annual reports, and key financial ratios, you can gauge the company's profitability, liquidity, solvency, and efficiency. This information is vital for making investment decisions, benchmarking performance against competitors, and assessing the company's ability to weather economic downturns or market fluctuations.

3. Identifying Growth Opportunities: Company research can help you identify growth opportunities within the organization. By analyzing market trends, competitive landscapes, customer preferences, and industry developments, you can pinpoint areas where the company can expand its reach, launch new products or services, or enter new markets. Understanding

these growth opportunities can inform strategic planning and decision-making, leading to sustainable business growth.

4. Assessing Competitor Landscape: Researching a company also involves analyzing its competitors to understand their strengths, weaknesses, market positioning, and strategies. By conducting competitive analysis, you can identify potential threats, benchmark your performance against industry peers, and uncover opportunities for differentiation. This competitive intelligence is valuable for developing effective marketing strategies, improving product offerings, and staying ahead of industry trends.

5. Preparing for Job Interviews: For job seekers, researching a company is crucial for preparing for job interviews. By familiarizing yourself with the company's products, services, culture, and recent developments, you can demonstrate your interest and knowledge during the interview process. Employers appreciate candidates who have done their homework and can articulate how their skills and experiences align with the company's goals and values.

6. Building Strategic Partnerships: When seeking to establish strategic partnerships with other companies, thorough research is essential. By understanding the potential partner's business model, market positioning, customer base, and objectives, you can identify synergies, assess compatibility, and negotiate mutually beneficial terms. Effective partnership research can lead to collaborations that drive innovation, enhance competitiveness, and create value for both parties.

7. Mitigating Risks: Researching a company can also help you identify potential risks and challenges that may impact your business relationships or investment decisions. By conducting due diligence on key stakeholders, regulatory compliance, legal issues, and reputation management, you can mitigate risks and avoid costly mistakes. This proactive approach to risk management can safeguard your interests and support long-term sustainability.

Overall, company research plays a critical role in various aspects of business, from strategic planning and decision-making to risk management and relationship building. By investing time and effort in gathering relevant information about a company, individuals and organizations can make informed choices that align with their goals, values, and priorities.

Strategies for Gathering Information

Effective company research requires a systematic approach and a mix of strategies to gather accurate, up-to-date, and relevant information. Here are some strategies that can help you gather valuable insights about a company:

1. Utilize Official Sources: Start your research by exploring the company's official website, where you can find essential information such as its history, mission statement, products or services, leadership team, locations, and contact details. Official sources provide a reliable foundation for your research and offer insights into how the company presents itself to the public.

2. Review Financial Reports: To assess the company's financial

health and performance, review its financial reports, including annual reports, quarterly earnings releases, and SEC filings. Pay attention to key financial metrics such as revenue, profit margins, cash flow, debt levels, and growth rates. Analyzing financial reports can help you evaluate the company's stability, profitability, and growth prospects.

3. Monitor News and Press Releases: Stay updated on the latest news, press releases, and media coverage related to the company. By monitoring news sources, industry publications, and social media channels, you can track important developments, such as product launches, partnerships, acquisitions, leadership changes, legal disputes, or financial milestones. This real-time information can provide valuable insights into the company's current activities and strategic direction.

4. Conduct SWOT Analysis: Perform a SWOT analysis (Strengths, Weaknesses, Opportunities, Threats) to assess the company's internal capabilities and external environment. Identify the company's core strengths, competitive advantages, areas for improvement, growth opportunities, and potential risks or challenges. A SWOT analysis can help you gain a holistic view of the company's position in the market and inform your strategic decisions.

5. Explore Industry Reports and Analyst Insights: Consult industry reports, market research studies, and analyst insights to gain a broader perspective on the company's industry landscape and competitive dynamics. Industry reports provide valuable data on market trends, customer preferences, regulatory changes, and technological advancements that may impact the com-

pany's performance. Analyst insights can offer expert opinions on the company's prospects, risks, and valuation.

6. Engage with Current and Former Employees: Reach out to current and former employees of the company to gather firsthand insights into its culture, work environment, leadership style, employee satisfaction, and growth opportunities. Networking with employees through professional platforms like LinkedIn or industry events can help you gain valuable perspectives that may not be available through official channels. Employees can provide candid feedback and insider knowledge that can inform your decision-making.

7. Attend Industry Events and Conferences: Participate in industry events, conferences, trade shows, and networking events where the company is likely to have a presence. These gatherings provide opportunities to interact with company representatives, industry experts, customers, and competitors, gaining firsthand knowledge about the company's products, services, strategies, and market positioning. Networking at industry events can also help you build relationships and stay informed about industry trends.

8. Utilize Online Databases and Tools: Leverage online databases, research tools, and business intelligence platforms to access a wealth of data and insights about the company. Platforms like Bloomberg, Reuters, Hoovers, and Crunchbase offer company profiles, financial data, news alerts, market analysis, and competitive intelligence that can support your research efforts. These tools provide a convenient way to access and analyze information efficiently.

9. Seek Customer Feedback and Reviews: Monitor customer feedback, reviews, ratings, and testimonials about the company's products or services on websites, social media platforms, and review sites. Understanding customer perceptions, preferences, and satisfaction levels can provide valuable insights into the company's brand reputation, product quality, customer service, and competitive positioning. Customer feedback can help you assess the company's market perception and identify areas for improvement.

10. Engage with Industry Experts and Consultants: Consult with industry experts, consultants, advisors, or mentors who have deep knowledge and experience in the company's industry sector. Industry experts can offer valuable insights, trends, and best practices that can inform your research and decision-making process. Engaging with experienced professionals can help you gain a deeper understanding of the industry landscape and navigate complex challenges more effectively.

11. Conduct Competitor Analysis: Analyze the company's key competitors to understand their strengths, weaknesses, market share, pricing strategies, product offerings, and customer base. By comparing the company's performance against its competitors, you can identify areas of competitive advantage, market opportunities, and potential threats. Competitor analysis provides valuable benchmarking data that can guide your strategic planning and positioning.

12. Use Social Media Listening Tools: Monitor social media channels, forums, and online communities using social media listening tools to track conversations, trends, and sentiment

related to the company. Social media monitoring helps you uncover public perceptions, industry trends, customer preferences, and emerging issues that may impact the company's reputation or business objectives. By analyzing social media data, you can gain actionable insights into consumer behavior, market dynamics, and brand sentiment.

In conclusion, researching a company is a fundamental aspect of business strategy, decision-making, and relationship building. By understanding the importance of company research and employing effective strategies for gathering information, individuals and organizations can gain valuable insights, mitigate risks, capitalize on opportunities, and make informed choices that drive success and growth. Whether you are a job seeker, investor, entrepreneur, student, or business professional, mastering the art of company research can enhance your competitiveness, broaden your perspective, and empower you to navigate the dynamic business landscape with confidence and clarity.

5

Understanding the Role

Crafting an effective elevator pitch is a crucial skill in the professional world. Whether you are attending a networking event, a job fair, or just meeting new people in your industry, having a well-prepared elevator pitch can make a lasting impression. An elevator pitch is a brief, persuasive speech that you can use to spark interest in what you do or what you have to offer. It should be concise, engaging, and provide a quick overview of who you are and what you bring to the table.

1. Crafting a Concise Self-Introduction

Crafting a concise self-introduction is the first step in preparing your elevator pitch. This introduction should be around 30 seconds to 2 minutes long, as this is the typical amount of time you might have in an elevator with someone. The goal is to grab the listener's attention and communicate who you are and what you do effectively.

Elements of a Self-Introduction:
  1. Introduction: Start by introducing yourself with your name

and briefly mention your current position or role.

- Example: "Hi, I'm Sarah Jones, a marketing specialist at XYZ Company."

2. Professional Background: Provide a brief overview of your professional background or experience.

- Example: "I have over five years of experience in digital marketing and have worked with a diverse range of clients."

3. Skills and Expertise: Highlight your key skills and expertise that are relevant to the listener.

- Example: "I specialize in social media marketing strategies and have a proven track record of increasing engagement and conversions."

4. Passion and Motivation: Share a bit about what motivates you and why you are passionate about your work.

- Example: "I am passionate about using data-driven insights to create effective marketing campaigns that drive results."

5. Unique Selling Proposition (USP): Mention what sets you apart from others in your field.

- Example: "I have a keen eye for detail and a creative approach to problem-solving that helps me deliver unique and innovative solutions."

6. Call to Action (CTA): End your self-introduction with a call to action, such as offering to connect further or suggesting a potential collaboration.

- Example: "I would love to discuss how we can work together to take your marketing efforts to the next level. Let's connect after the event."

2. Highlighting Your Key Qualifications

Highlighting your key qualifications is essential in making your elevator pitch impactful and memorable. This part of the pitch should focus on the specific skills, experiences, achievements, and credentials that set you apart and make you a valuable asset in your field.

Tips for Highlighting Key Qualifications:

1. Relevance: Focus on qualifications that are most relevant to the person or context you are addressing. Tailor your qualifications based on the industry, role, or individual you are speaking to.

2. Quantify Achievements: Where possible, include quantifiable achievements or results to demonstrate the impact of your qualifications.
   - Example: "I increased sales by 30% through the implementation of a new customer retention strategy."

3. Credentials and Certifications: Mention any relevant certifications, awards, or credentials that showcase your expertise and credibility in your field.
   - Example: "I am a certified project management professional with a track record of delivering projects on time and within budget."

4. Soft Skills: Don't forget to highlight your soft skills, such as communication, leadership, teamwork, and problem-solving abilities. These skills are equally important in showcasing your

overall capabilities.
- Example: "I have strong interpersonal skills that allow me to effectively collaborate with cross-functional teams and stakeholders."

5. Industry Knowledge: Demonstrate your industry knowledge and understanding by mentioning any specific trends, challenges, or innovations that you are familiar with.
- Example: "I stay updated on the latest trends in digital marketing and have a deep understanding of how to leverage emerging technologies for brand growth."

Elevator Pitch Example:

Now, let's put all these elements together to create a sample elevator pitch that effectively showcases both a concise self-introduction and highlights key qualifications:

"Hi, I'm Alex Martinez, a seasoned project manager with a background in leading cross-functional teams to successful project delivery. Over the past eight years, I have managed complex projects in various industries, consistently meeting deadlines and exceeding client expectations. My expertise lies in Agile project management methodologies, where I have facilitated seamless communication and collaboration among team members to ensure project success. I recently received the 'Project Manager of the Year' award for my role in implementing a streamlined project management process that led to a 20% increase in team productivity. I am passionate about fostering a culture of innovation and continuous improvement in every project I undertake. I would love to explore how my skills and experience can contribute to the success of your upcoming initiatives. Let's connect to discuss potential opportunities for collaboration."

Conclusion

Crafting a compelling elevator pitch requires careful thought and preparation. By focusing on creating a concise self-introduction and highlighting your key qualifications, you can effectively communicate your value proposition and make a lasting impression on your audience. Remember to tailor your elevator pitch to different situations and audiences to maximize its impact. With practice and refinement, your elevator pitch can become a powerful tool for networking, job interviews, or any professional interaction where you want to showcase your skills and expertise effectively.

6

Preparing Your Elevator Pitch

Common Interview Questions and Strategies for Effective Answers

Interviews are an essential part of the job application process, providing employers with the opportunity to evaluate candidates beyond their resumes. In many cases, applicants may have similar qualifications on paper, making the interview crucial for standing out. To prepare for interviews, it's important to anticipate common questions and develop strategies for answering them effectively. In this guide, we will delve into various frequently asked interview questions and provide tips on how to respond to them to make a lasting impression on your potential employer.

Overview of Common Interview Questions

1. Tell Me About Yourself

This open-ended question is often used as an icebreaker to allow candidates to introduce themselves. While it might seem simple, many candidates struggle with where to start and how much detail to provide. The key here is to provide a concise summary of your professional background, skills, and experiences relevant to the position you are applying for. Avoid sharing personal information not related to the job.

Example:

"I have a background in marketing with five years of experience working in various industries such as technology and healthcare. I specialize in digital marketing strategies, and I have a proven track record of increasing brand visibility and engagement for my previous employers."

2. Why Do You Want to Work Here?

Employers want to know what motivates you to join their organization specifically. To answer this question effectively, research the company beforehand and identify key factors that appeal to you, such as its culture, values, or projects. Show enthusiasm and a genuine interest in the company's mission and vision.

Example:

"I have always been impressed by your company's commitment to innovation and sustainability. Your recent project on developing eco-friendly products aligns with my values, and I believe my skills in product development can contribute to your mission."

3. What Are Your Strengths and Weaknesses?

This classic question assesses your self-awareness and ability to reflect on your professional traits. When discussing your strengths, focus on valuable skills and qualities that are relevant to the job. When addressing weaknesses, be honest but also share how you are working to improve them.

Example:

"One of my strengths is my ability to communicate effectively with diverse team members, which helps streamline projects and enhance collaboration. As for weaknesses, I sometimes have a tendency to be overly detail-oriented, but I have been working on delegating tasks more efficiently."

4. Describe a Challenging Situation and How You Overcame It

Behavioral questions like this one aim to assess your problem-solving skills and resilience. When sharing a challenging experience, structure your response using the STAR method (Situation, Task, Action, Result) to provide a comprehensive answer.

Example:

"During a time-sensitive project, our team faced unexpected delays due to technical issues. I took the lead in troubleshooting the problem, coordinating with the IT department to find solutions, and ultimately, we were able to meet the deadline with minimal impact on the project's outcome."

5. Where Do You See Yourself in Five Years?

Employers ask this question to gauge your long-term career goals and ambitions. While you may not have a detailed plan for the next five years, it's essential to demonstrate your commitment to growth and professional development. Tailor your response to show how the role you are applying for fits into your career trajectory.

Example:

"In five years, I see myself taking on a leadership role within the company, leveraging my expertise to mentor and guide junior team members. I am excited about the opportunity to grow alongside the organization and contribute to its success."

6. Why Should We Hire You?

This question allows you to highlight your unique selling points and what sets you apart from other candidates. Focus on your skills, experiences, and achievements that directly align with the job requirements. Be confident in showcasing what you can bring to the role and the company.

Example:

"Based on my extensive experience in project management and my track record of delivering successful outcomes on complex projects, I believe I can immediately add value to your team. My ability to effectively collaborate with cross-functional stakeholders and drive results sets me apart as a candidate."

7. Do You Have Any Questions for Us?

At the end of an interview, you are typically given the chance to ask questions. Use this opportunity to demonstrate your interest in the role and the company by asking insightful questions about the team, projects, or company culture. Avoid questions that solely focus on salary or benefits.

Example:

"I am curious about the team dynamics within the department and how collaboration is encouraged among team members. Could you provide some insights into the current and upcoming projects that the team is working on?"

Strategies for Answering Interview Questions Effectively

1. Prepare and Practice

One of the most effective strategies for answering interview questions is thorough preparation. Research the company, review the job description, and anticipate potential questions based on the role. Practice your responses out loud or with a friend to gain confidence and refine your answers.

2. Focus on Relevant Examples

When answering behavioral questions or describing your skills, always provide specific examples from your past experiences. Use the STAR method to structure your responses, highlighting the situation, task, actions you took, and the results achieved. This approach adds credibility to your answers and demonstrates your abilities in action.

3. Tailor Your Responses

Each interview question presents an opportunity to showcase your fit for the role and the company. Tailor your responses by aligning your skills, experiences, and achievements with the job requirements and company culture. Show how your background uniquely qualifies you for the position.

4. Be Honest and Authentic

While it's important to present yourself in the best light during an interview, avoid exaggerating or providing false information. Be honest about your experiences, skills, and motivations. Authenticity builds trust with the interviewer and allows them to get a genuine sense of who you are as a candidate.

5. Demonstrate Enthusiasm

Show genuine enthusiasm for the role and the company throughout the interview. Express your passion for the industry, your eagerness to contribute, and your interest in the organization's goals. Employers are more likely to remember candidates who demonstrate genuine excitement and a positive attitude.

6. Stay Positive and Professional

Even when discussing challenging situations or addressing weaknesses, maintain a positive and professional demeanor. Focus on how you overcame obstacles or learned from past experiences to grow and improve. Avoid speaking negatively about previous employers or colleagues, as this reflects poorly on your professionalism.

7. Ask Clarifying Questions

If you encounter a question that is unclear or ambiguous, don't hesitate to ask for clarification. It's better to seek additional information to ensure you understand the question fully and provide an appropriate response. Asking thoughtful questions also demonstrates your critical thinking skills and engagement.

8. Practice Active Listening

Effective communication is a two-way street, so practice active listening during the interview. Pay attention to the interviewer's questions, ask for clarification if needed, and respond thoughtfully. Demonstrating good listening skills shows that you are engaged and interested in the conversation.

9. Showcase Your Problem-Solving Skills

Many interview questions are designed to evaluate your problem-solving abilities and critical thinking. When discussing challenging situations or providing examples of past accomplishments, emphasize your problem-solving skills and the strategies you used to overcome obstacles. Employers value candidates who can think creatively and handle challenges effectively.

10. Follow Up With a Thank-You Note

After the interview, send a thank-you note to the interviewer expressing your appreciation for the opportunity to discuss the role. Reiterate your interest in the position and briefly mention key points from the interview that highlight your qualifications. A well-crafted thank-you note can leave a positive impression and reinforce your enthusiasm for the role.

In conclusion, preparing for common interview questions and developing effective strategies for answering them can significantly enhance your performance during job interviews. By anticipating potential questions, tailoring your responses to showcase your skills and experiences, and demonstrating enthusiasm and professionalism, you can make a strong impression on your potential employer. Remember to practice, stay authentic, and approach each question with confidence and a positive attitude. Good luck in your upcoming interviews!

7

Common Interview Questions

Common Interview Questions and Strategies for Answering Effectively

In the competitive job market, preparing for a job interview is crucial to make a lasting impression on the interviewer. Knowing the common interview questions and how to answer them effectively can significantly improve your chances of securing the job. This article provides an overview of some of the most common interview questions and strategies for answering them effectively.

Overview of Common Interview Questions

1. Tell me about yourself
   - This is often the first question in an interview and an opportunity to introduce yourself to the interviewer. Keep your response concise, focusing on your professional background, relevant experiences, and skills.
   - Example: "I am a marketing professional with five years

of experience in digital marketing. I have a strong track record of developing successful marketing campaigns for various clients."

2. What are your strengths and weaknesses?
   - Highlight your strengths that are relevant to the job you are applying for. When discussing weaknesses, focus on areas where you have identified opportunities for growth and improvement.
   - Example: "One of my strengths is my ability to work well under pressure and deliver results within tight deadlines. As for weaknesses, I have been working on improving my public speaking skills through practice and training."

3. Why do you want to work for this company?
   - Demonstrate your knowledge of the company by mentioning specific reasons why you are interested in working there. Research the company's values, mission, and culture to tailor your response.
   - Example: "I am impressed by your company's commitment to innovation and sustainability, which aligns with my own values. I believe that my skills and experience would be a great fit for the team and contribute to the company's success."

4. Tell me about a time when you faced a challenge at work and how you overcame it
   - Use the STAR method (Situation, Task, Action, Result) to structure your response. Describe a specific challenge you encountered, the actions you took to address it, and the outcome of your efforts.
   - Example: "In my previous role, I was tasked with launching a new product within a tight timeline. I collaborated with cross-

functional teams, set clear milestones, and communicated effectively to ensure the successful launch of the product ahead of schedule."

5. Where do you see yourself in five years?
   - Show your ambition and long-term career goals by discussing how you envision your professional growth within the company. Emphasize your commitment to personal development and continuous learning.
   - Example: "In five years, I see myself taking on a more leadership role within the company, leading a team of marketing professionals and contributing to the strategic growth of the organization."

6. Why should we hire you?
   - Highlight your unique qualifications, skills, and experiences that make you the ideal candidate for the job. Demonstrate your value proposition and how you can contribute to the company's success.
   - Example: "I believe my proven track record in project management, strong analytical skills, and ability to work collaboratively with diverse teams make me a valuable asset to your organization. I am confident that I can make a significant impact and drive results in this role."

7. Tell me about a time when you had to work with a difficult colleague or client
   - Demonstrate your ability to handle conflict and communicate effectively in challenging situations. Describe how you approached the situation, resolved conflicts, and maintained a professional relationship.

- Example: "I once had to work with a colleague who had a different work style than mine, leading to misunderstandings and delays in our project. I initiated a candid conversation with my colleague to address our differences, set clear expectations, and established a workflow that allowed us to work efficiently and successfully complete the project."

Strategies for Answering Effectively

1. Prepare and practice
   - Research the company, review the job description, and prepare examples that showcase your skills and experiences. Practice answering common interview questions with a friend or a mentor to build confidence and refine your responses.

2. Tailor your responses
   - Customize your answers to align with the job requirements and the company's culture. Highlight your relevant experiences, skills, and achievements that demonstrate your fit for the role.

3. Use the STAR method
   - Structure your responses using the STAR method to provide clear and concise examples of your problem-solving skills, achievements, and experiences. This method helps you communicate your stories effectively and showcase your abilities to the interviewer.

4. Be authentic and positive
   - Be genuine in your responses and showcase your enthusiasm for the role and the company. Maintain a positive attitude throughout the interview, and demonstrate your passion for

the work you do.

5. Showcase your soft skills
 - Highlight your soft skills, such as communication, teamwork, problem-solving, and adaptability, as these are often crucial for success in the workplace. Provide examples that demonstrate how you have utilized these skills in previous roles.

6. Ask questions
 - Prepare thoughtful questions to ask the interviewer about the company, the team, or the role. This demonstrates your interest in the position and allows you to gather more information to assess if the role is the right fit for you.

7. Practice active listening
 - Pay attention to the interviewer's questions and cues, and respond thoughtfully. Take time to understand the question before providing your response, and ask for clarification if needed.

8. Follow up after the interview
 - Send a thank-you email to the interviewer expressing your gratitude for the opportunity to interview and reiterating your interest in the position. This gesture demonstrates professionalism and keeps you on the interviewer's radar.

In conclusion, preparing for common interview questions and using effective strategies to answer them can enhance your performance in job interviews and increase your likelihood of securing the job. By showcasing your skills, experiences, and enthusiasm for the role, you can leave a lasting impression on the interviewer and position yourself as a strong candidate for the position. Remember to tailor your responses, practice your answers, and demonstrate your value to the company to stand out in the interview process.

8

Behavioral Interview Questions

Behavioral interview questions are a common way for employers to evaluate a candidate's past experiences and behavior in various situations. Rather than focusing solely on hypothetical situations or technical knowledge, behavioral interview questions aim to reveal how a candidate has handled specific scenarios in the past. By understanding how a candidate has approached challenges, interacted with others, and achieved results in previous roles, employers can gain insights into the candidate's potential fit within their organization.

In this deep dive, we will explore the concept of behavioral interview questions, discuss the reasons behind their popularity, and provide insights into how candidates can effectively respond to these questions using the STAR method. Additionally, we will provide examples of common behavioral interview questions and demonstrate how the STAR method can be applied to formulate structured and compelling responses.

Understanding Behavioral Interview Questions

Behavioral interview questions are based on the premise that past behavior is a strong indicator of future performance. By asking candidates to describe specific examples of how they have handled challenges or situations in the past, interviewers aim to gain a deeper understanding of the candidate's skills, competencies, and approach to problem-solving.

These questions are typically designed to assess various aspects of a candidate's behavior, including their communication skills, decision-making abilities, problem-solving techniques, teamwork, leadership potential, adaptability, and more. By focusing on real-life examples rather than theoretical responses, behavioral interview questions provide valuable insights into how a candidate is likely to perform in a given role.

Employers value behavioral interview questions for several reasons:

1. Relevance: Behavioral interview questions are highly effective in predicting a candidate's future performance because they are based on actual experiences rather than hypothetical scenarios.

2. Consistency: By asking all candidates the same set of behavioral questions, interviewers ensure a consistent evaluation process that allows for fair comparisons.

3. Behavioral indicators: These questions reveal important behavioral indicators such as problem-solving skills, interpersonal abilities, adaptability, resilience, and leadership potential.

4. Authenticity: Candidates' responses to behavioral questions

provide genuine insights into their personalities, work ethic, and approach to challenges.

5. Structured evaluation: By structuring questions around specific behavioral competencies, interviewers can assess candidates objectively and make more informed hiring decisions.

Using the STAR Method to Respond

When responding to behavioral interview questions, candidates can use the STAR method to provide structured, concise, and compelling answers. The STAR method is an acronym that stands for Situation, Task, Action, and Result. By structuring responses according to these four components, candidates can effectively communicate their experiences and showcase relevant skills to the interviewer.

Here is a breakdown of each component of the STAR method:

1. Situation: Begin by setting the context for your response. Describe the situation or challenge you faced, providing the interviewer with a clear understanding of the context in which the scenario unfolded.

2. Task: Outline the specific task or objective you were trying to accomplish in that situation. Clearly articulate what was expected of you and what goals you were working towards.

3. Action: Detail the actions you took to address the challenge or situation. Focus on your role in the process, highlighting the specific steps you took and the strategies you implemented to

achieve your goals.

4. Result: Finally, share the outcome of your actions. Describe the results of your efforts, including any impact your actions had on the situation or organization. Whenever possible, quantify your achievements or outcomes to provide concrete evidence of your success.

By structuring your responses using the STAR method, you can ensure that your answers are well-organized, easy to follow, and focused on highlighting your skills and accomplishments effectively.

Examples of Behavioral Interview Questions

Let's explore some common behavioral interview questions along with examples of how candidates can respond using the STAR method:

1. Describe a time when you had to work under pressure to meet a tight deadline. How did you handle the situation?

- Situation: While working at Company X, I was assigned a project with an urgent deadline due to unforeseen circumstances. The project required me to deliver a detailed report within 48 hours.

- Task: My task was to analyze complex data, prepare a comprehensive report, and present my findings to the management team within the specified timeframe.

- Action: To manage the pressure and meet the deadline, I prioritized my tasks, created a detailed timeline, and communicated with team members to streamline the process. I worked long hours, stayed focused, and remained organized throughout the project.

- Result: As a result of my efforts, I successfully completed the report ahead of schedule and presented it to the management team, receiving positive feedback for my efficiency and dedication. The project's success reinforced my ability to perform well under pressure and deliver high-quality work in demanding situations.

2. Tell me about a time when you had to resolve a conflict within a team. How did you approach the situation?

- Situation: While working on a collaborative project at Company Y, tensions arose between team members due to differing opinions on the project approach, leading to a potential conflict.

- Task: My task was to address the conflict, facilitate communication, and find a resolution that would allow the team to work together effectively towards the project goals.

- Action: I decided to schedule a team meeting to openly discuss the issues and understand each team member's perspective. I actively listened to their concerns, encouraged constructive dialogue, and facilitated a brainstorming session to generate solutions. I collaborated with team members to develop a compromise that aligned with everyone's interests.

- Result: By proactively addressing the conflict and fostering effective communication, I was able to resolve the tensions within the team and create a more collaborative and harmonious working environment. The successful resolution of the conflict strengthened team dynamics and improved overall project outcomes.

3. Describe a challenging project you were involved in. What obstacles did you encounter, and how did you overcome them?

- Situation: During my time at Company Z, I was tasked with leading a high-stakes project that involved significant technical complexities and tight deadlines. The project's success was critical to the company's strategic goals.

- Task: My task was to coordinate cross-functional teams, manage project timelines and deliverables, and ensure the project aligned with stakeholders' expectations.

- Action: Despite facing challenges such as resource constraints and unexpected technical issues, I remained focused on problem-solving and collaboration. I conducted regular meetings with team members to address obstacles proactively, adjusted project timelines when necessary, and leveraged my expertise to provide guidance and support to team members.

- Result: Through my strategic leadership and persistent efforts, I successfully navigated the project through challenges, met all deliverable milestones, and ultimately achieved project success. The project's positive outcomes demonstrated my ability to adapt to changing circumstances, resolve complex issues, and deliver results under challenging conditions.

These examples illustrate how candidates can effectively respond to behavioral interview questions using the STAR method. By structuring their responses around specific situations, tasks, actions, and results, candidates can provide compelling and relevant anecdotes that showcase their skills, competencies, and experiences to potential employers.

In conclusion, behavioral interview questions offer valuable insights into a candidate's past behavior, skills, and capabilities, helping employers assess their suitability for a given role. By using the STAR method to respond to these questions, candidates can present structured, concise, and impactful answers that highlight their qualifications and strengths effectively. Mastering the art of responding to behavioral interview questions can significantly enhance a candidate's chances of success during the interview process and ultimately secure their desired position.

9

Mock Interviews

Mock Interviews: Importance and Effective Practices

Mock interviews are simulated job interviews where candidates practice answering commonly asked questions and receive feedback on their performance. This exercise is crucial in preparing candidates for actual interviews by helping them refine their responses, boost their confidence, and identify areas for improvement. In this discussion, we will delve into the importance of mock interviews and provide tips for conducting them effectively.

Importance of Mock Interviews

1. Preparation: Mock interviews allow candidates to prepare for the real thing. By simulating interview scenarios, candidates can become familiar with common questions, practice articulating their experiences and skills, and develop strategies to handle difficult inquiries.

2. Confidence Building: One of the main benefits of mock interviews is boosting candidates' confidence. By practicing in a low-stakes environment, candidates can overcome nervousness and develop a sense of assurance in their abilities.

3. Feedback and Improvement: Mock interviews provide valuable feedback to candidates. Interviewers can offer constructive criticism on aspects such as body language, communication skills, and responses to questions. This feedback enables candidates to identify their strengths and weaknesses, allowing them to make improvements before the actual interview.

4. Enhanced Performance: Through repeated practice, candidates can refine their responses, polish their communication skills, and develop a compelling narrative that highlights their qualifications. This preparation often leads to improved performance during real interviews.

5. Reduction of Interview Anxiety: Interview anxiety is common among job seekers. Mock interviews help alleviate this anxiety by familiarizing candidates with the interview process, increasing their comfort level, and reducing the fear of the unknown.

6. Time Management: Mock interviews also help candidates manage their time effectively during interviews. By practicing responses and refining their delivery, candidates can learn to structure their answers concisely and make the most of the limited time available in interviews.

Tips for Conducting Mock Interviews Effectively

1. Choose a Skilled Interviewer: Select an experienced interviewer who is knowledgeable about the job market and common interview practices. This individual can provide valuable insights and constructive feedback to help candidates improve.

2. Create a Realistic Environment: Set up the mock interview environment to mirror a real interview scenario. Dress professionally, gather necessary materials, and maintain a professional demeanor throughout the session.

3. Use Relevant Questions: Tailor the questions asked during the mock interview to the specific job or industry the candidate is targeting. This customization ensures that candidates practice responding to inquiries relevant to their field.

4. Provide Detailed Feedback: After the mock interview, offer detailed feedback to the candidate. Highlight areas of strength and areas for improvement, providing specific examples and suggestions for enhancement.

5. Encourage Self-Reflection: Encourage candidates to reflect on their performance during the mock interview. Ask them to identify areas they believe they excelled in and areas where they feel they need to improve. This self-assessment fosters a proactive approach to skill development.

6. Practice Behavioral Questions: Behavioral questions are commonly used in interviews to assess a candidate's past behavior and experiences. Include these types of questions in mock interviews to help candidates prepare compelling anecdotes that demonstrate their skills and qualities.

7. Focus on Non-Verbal Communication: Pay attention to candidates' non-verbal communication cues during the mock interview. Body language, eye contact, and posture play a significant role in interviews, and practicing these aspects can enhance candidates' overall performance.

8. Recreate Stressful Situations: Introduce challenging scenarios or unexpected questions during the mock interview to help candidates practice thinking on their feet and remaining composed under pressure. This simulation can prepare candidates for handling difficult moments during real interviews.

9. Offer Opportunities for Repeat Practice: Encourage candidates to participate in multiple mock interviews to refine their skills further. Repetition helps candidates become more comfortable with the process and fine-tune their responses.

10. Utilize Video Recording: Consider recording the mock interviews to provide candidates with a playback of their performance. This visual feedback can offer valuable insights into areas such as body language, tone of voice, and overall presentation.

In conclusion, mock interviews are invaluable tools for job seekers seeking to improve their interview skills and enhance their chances of success. By practicing in a simulated environment, candidates can refine their responses, build confidence, and receive constructive feedback to help them excel in real interviews. When conducted effectively, mock interviews serve as critical components of interview preparation, empowering candidates to showcase their qualifications and secure their desired positions.

10

Dress and Body Language

Dress and body language play crucial roles in how we are perceived by others, especially in professional settings. Both aspects can influence our credibility, confidence, and professionalism. In this discussion, we will delve deep into the importance of professional attire guidelines and the significance of positive body language in various professional settings.

Professional Attire Guidelines

Professional attire refers to the clothing and accessories that individuals wear in the workplace or during professional interactions. Dressing appropriately is essential as it enhances one's credibility, creates a positive first impression, and promotes a sense of professionalism. Here are some guidelines to consider when selecting professional attire:

1. Understand the Dress Code: Different workplaces have varying dress codes, ranging from formal to casual. It is essential to understand and adhere to the specific dress code of

your workplace or industry.

2. Dress for the Occasion: Consider the nature of the event or meeting you will be attending when selecting your attire. Dress one level above the expected dress code to demonstrate respect and professionalism.

3. Fit and Tailoring: Ensure that your clothing fits well and is properly tailored to your body shape. Ill-fitting clothing can appear unprofessional and impact your overall appearance.

4. Colors and Patterns: Choose colors and patterns that are professional and appropriate for the workplace. Neutral colors such as black, navy, gray, and white are safe choices, while subtle patterns can add interest without being distracting.

5. Avoid Overly Casual Attire: Stay away from overly casual clothing such as ripped jeans, shorts, flip-flops, or t-shirts unless it is explicitly allowed in your workplace.

6. Footwear and Accessories: Pay attention to your choice of footwear and accessories. Opt for closed-toe shoes in neutral colors and limit the use of accessories to maintain a professional look.

7. Grooming and Personal Hygiene: Maintain good grooming habits and ensure your clothing is clean and well-pressed. Pay attention to your personal hygiene as it contributes to your overall appearance.

8. Be Mindful of Cultural Sensitivities: In a diverse workplace, be

mindful of cultural sensitivities and dress codes. Avoid clothing that may be offensive to others and respect different cultural norms.

9. Invest in Quality Pieces: Invest in quality clothing pieces that are versatile and durable. Quality clothing lasts longer, fits better, and projects a more professional image.

Examples of Professional Attire:

1. Business Formal: For a business formal setting, men can wear a tailored suit in navy or charcoal gray with a white dress shirt and a conservative tie. Women can opt for a tailored pantsuit or a knee-length skirt suit paired with a blouse or button-down shirt.

2. Business Casual: In a business casual environment, men can wear dress pants paired with a collared shirt or a sweater. Women can choose to wear a blouse with dress pants or a knee-length skirt with a cardigan.

3. Creative Industry: In a creative industry, professionals have more flexibility in their attire. Men can wear a casual blazer with dark jeans and a button-down shirt. Women can opt for a stylish dress or a blouse paired with tailored pants.

4. Client Meetings: When meeting with clients, it is essential to dress more formally to convey professionalism and respect. Men can wear a suit with a tie, while women can opt for a tailored dress or pantsuit.

By following these guidelines and choosing appropriate attire for various professional situations, individuals can create a positive impression and enhance their credibility in the workplace.

Tips for Positive Body Language

Body language is a powerful form of communication that can influence how others perceive us. Positive body language can convey confidence, credibility, and professionalism, while negative body language can create barriers to effective communication. Here are some tips to help you project positive body language in professional settings:

1. Maintain Eye Contact: Eye contact is a fundamental aspect of positive body language. It demonstrates attentiveness, confidence, and interest in the conversation. When speaking or listening, make sure to maintain appropriate eye contact with the person you are communicating with.

2. Posture: Good posture is key to projecting confidence and professionalism. Stand or sit up straight, with your shoulders back and head held high. Avoid slouching or leaning excessively, as it can convey disinterest or lack of confidence.

3. Smile: A genuine smile can go a long way in creating a positive connection with others. Smiling conveys warmth, approachability, and positivity. However, be mindful of the context and ensure that your smile is appropriate for the situation.

4. Hand Gestures: Use purposeful hand gestures to emphasize your points and add energy to your communication. Avoid overly

distracting or repetitive hand movements, as they can detract from your message.

5. Mirroring: Mirroring the body language of the person you are communicating with can help create rapport and establish a connection. Subtly match their gestures, posture, and facial expressions to build a sense of harmony in the interaction.

6. Personal Space: Respect personal space boundaries when interacting with others. Standing too close can be perceived as intrusive, while standing too far away may create a sense of aloofness. Maintain a comfortable distance based on cultural norms and individual preferences.

7. Handshake: A firm, confident handshake is crucial in professional interactions. A weak handshake can convey hesitance or lack of confidence, while an overly aggressive handshake can seem domineering. Aim for a balanced and firm handshake to establish a positive first impression.

8. Facial Expressions: Be mindful of your facial expressions as they can convey a range of emotions to others. Maintain a neutral or positive facial expression to demonstrate engagement and interest in the conversation.

9. Active Listening: Engage in active listening by nodding, maintaining eye contact, and responding appropriately to the speaker. Show interest in the conversation by asking questions and providing feedback to demonstrate your attentiveness.

10. Confidence: Confidence is key to projecting positive body

language. Believe in yourself, maintain a strong posture, and present yourself with assurance and poise. Confidence is contagious and can inspire trust and respect in others.

Examples of Positive Body Language:

1. Engaged Posture: Sitting up straight with shoulders back and leaning slightly forward indicates engagement and interest in the conversation.

2. Open Gestures: Using open hand gestures while speaking conveys openness, honesty, and a willingness to communicate.

3. Nodding and Smiling: Nodding in agreement and smiling at appropriate moments shows that you are actively listening and engaged in the discussion.

4. Maintaining Eye Contact: Holding eye contact while speaking or listening demonstrates confidence, sincerity, and respect for the person you are conversing with.

5. Mirroring: Subtly mirroring the body language of the other person, such as matching their posture or gestures, can create a sense of connection and rapport.

6. Confident Handshake: Offering a firm handshake with eye contact and a smile establishes a positive first impression and conveys confidence and professionalism.

7. Relaxed Body Language: Avoiding tense or closed-off body language, such as crossed arms or fidgeting, helps create a sense

of ease and approachability in interactions.

By incorporating these tips and examples of positive body language into your professional interactions, you can enhance your communication skills, build rapport with others, and project a confident and professional image.

In conclusion, dress and body language are integral components of effective communication and professionalism in various professional settings. By following guidelines for professional attire and practicing positive body language tips, individuals can create a positive impression, communicate effectively, and establish strong relationships in the workplace. Remember that dressing appropriately and projecting positive body language not only enhance your personal brand but also contribute to your success and credibility in professional environments.

11

Interview Day

Preparing for an interview can be a stressful experience for many people. However, with proper preparation and strategy, you can increase your chances of success and feel more composed during the actual interview. In this guide, we will delve deeply into the key aspects of preparing for the day of the interview and explore effective strategies for staying composed throughout the process.

Preparing for the Day of the Interview

Preparing for the day of the interview is crucial as it sets the tone for how well you perform during the actual interview. Here are some key steps to help you prepare effectively:

Research the Company and the Role

Before the interview day, make sure to conduct thorough research on the company and the role you are applying for. Understanding the company's mission, values, products or services, and recent news can give you valuable insights that you can use during the interview. Similarly, familiarize yourself with the job description, required skills, and qualifications to tailor your responses accordingly.

Example:

If you are interviewing for a marketing position at a tech startup, research the company's target audience, marketing strategies, and any recent campaigns they have run. This information can help you demonstrate your understanding of their industry and needs during the interview.

Practice Common Interview Questions

Prepare responses to common interview questions such as "Tell me about yourself," "Why do you want to work here?" or "What are your strengths and weaknesses?" Practicing your responses can help you articulate your thoughts clearly and confidently during the interview. Additionally, consider preparing examples of past experiences or projects that demonstrate your skills and accomplishments.

Example:

If you are asked to provide an example of a challenging project you worked on, prepare a structured response that outlines the problem, your role in solving it, and the outcome. This can showcase your problem-solving skills and ability to work under pressure.

Dress Appropriately

Choose professional attire that is suitable for the company culture and industry. Dressing appropriately can create a positive first impression and show that you are serious about the opportunity. Make sure your clothes are clean, well-fitted, and free of wrinkles or stains. Pay attention to small details such as grooming, accessories, and shoes to ensure you look polished.

Example:

For a corporate job interview in a conservative industry such as finance or law, opt for a tailored suit, dress shirt, and closed-toe shoes. Avoid loud patterns or bright colors and keep your accessories minimal and understated. This demonstrates that you understand and respect the industry norms.

Plan Your Route and Arrive Early

Plan your route to the interview location in advance, taking into account factors such as traffic, parking, or public transportation schedules. Aim to arrive at least 10-15 minutes early to allow time for unexpected delays. Arriving early not only shows punctuality but also gives you a chance to relax, review your notes, and mentally prepare for the interview.

Example:

If your interview is in a different city, research the best mode of transportation and check for any potential construction or traffic delays. Arrive early at the interview location to avoid rushing and feeling flustered before the interview starts.

Prepare Questions for the Interviewer

Come prepared with thoughtful questions to ask the interviewer about the role, the team, or the company culture. Asking insightful questions not only demonstrates your interest in the position but also helps you gather valuable information to assess if the job is the right fit for you. Avoid asking questions that can be easily answered through basic research.

Example:

Ask the interviewer about the team's current projects, the company's long-term goals, or opportunities for professional development within the organization. These questions show your enthusiasm for the role and your interest in contributing to the company's success.

Strategies for Staying Composed

Interview nerves are natural, but with the right strategies, you can stay composed and perform at your best. Here are some effective strategies to help you manage stress and anxiety during the interview:

Practice Deep Breathing and Relaxation Techniques

Deep breathing exercises can help calm your nerves and reduce stress before and during the interview. Practice deep, diaphragmatic breathing by inhaling slowly through your nose, holding for a few seconds, and exhaling through your mouth. You can also try progressive muscle relaxation techniques to release tension from your body and promote a sense of calmness.

Example:

Before entering the interview room, take a few minutes to find a quiet spot and practice deep breathing exercises. Inhale deeply, hold for a count of four, and exhale slowly. Repeat this process several times to relax your mind and body.

Visualize a Positive Outcome

Visualizing a positive outcome can help boost your confidence and reduce anxiety. Imagine yourself excelling in the interview, answering questions confidently, and building rapport with the interviewer. Visualizing success can help shift your mindset from fear and doubt to a more optimistic and empowered state.

Example:
Close your eyes and visualize yourself walking into the interview room with a confident posture, making eye contact with the interviewer, and delivering your responses articulately. Imagine receiving positive feedback and feeling proud of your performance. This visualization exercise can help boost your self-assurance.

Focus on Your Body Language

Your body language communicates volumes during an interview, so pay attention to your posture, gestures, and facial expressions. Sit up straight, make eye contact, and offer a firm handshake to convey confidence and professionalism. Avoid fidgeting, crossing your arms, or displaying closed-off body language that may signal nervousness.

Example:

During the interview, maintain an open posture by sitting upright, leaning slightly forward to show engagement, and nodding to indicate understanding. Use hand gestures sparingly and maintain eye contact with the interviewer to demonstrate your attentiveness and interest.

Practice Mindful Listening

Active listening is a key skill during interviews, as it shows respect for the interviewer and allows you to respond thoughtfully to questions. Practice mindful listening by focusing on the interviewer's words, asking clarifying questions when needed, and demonstrating empathy and understanding in your responses. Avoid interrupting or formulating your response before the interviewer finishes speaking.

Example:

When the interviewer asks a question, listen attentively to their words without distractions. Take a moment to process the question, paraphrase it if necessary to ensure clarity, and respond in a concise and relevant manner. This demonstrates your communication skills and ability to engage in meaningful dialogue.

Embrace Positive Self-Talk

Positive self-talk involves using affirming statements to build confidence and counter negative thoughts or self-doubt. Replace limiting beliefs such as "I'm not good enough" or "I will fail" with positive affirmations like "I am prepared and capable" or "I have valuable skills to offer." Cultivating a positive and self-assured mindset can enhance your performance and resilience during the interview.

Example:

Before the interview, remind yourself of your achievements, strengths, and qualifications that make you a strong candidate. Repeat affirmations such as "I have worked hard to prepare for this opportunity" or "I am confident in my abilities." This positive self-talk can help boost your confidence and mental resilience.

Practice Mock Interviews

Mock interviews are a valuable tool for simulating the interview experience and receiving feedback on your performance. Practice with a friend, family member, mentor, or through online platforms that offer mock interview services. Use this opportunity to refine your responses, receive constructive criticism, and become more comfortable with the interview format.

Example:

Arrange a mock interview session with a trusted individual who can provide honest feedback and simulate real interview scenarios. Practice answering a variety of questions, receive feedback on your body language and communication style, and work on areas for improvement. This practice can help you feel more prepared and confident on the day of the actual interview.

Conclusion

Preparing for the day of the interview and staying composed

during the process are essential for showcasing your skills, qualifications, and suitability for the role. By conducting thorough research, practicing common interview questions, dressing appropriately, and arriving early, you can set yourself up for success. Additionally, employing strategies such as deep breathing, visualization, positive self-talk, and mindful listening can help you manage interview nerves and present your best self to the interviewer. Remember that interviews are not only about demonstrating your qualifications but also about showing your personality, professionalism, and enthusiasm for the opportunity. With ample preparation and effective strategies, you can navigate the interview process with confidence and composure, increasing your chances of securing the job you desire.

12

Follow-Up

Follow-up plays a crucial role in the job search process, especially after an interview. It allows candidates to demonstrate continued interest, professionalism, and gratitude, all of which can set them apart from other applicants. In this section, we will delve deeply into two key aspects of follow-up: sending a thank-you note and strategies for post-interview communication.

1. Sending a Thank-You Note

Sending a thank-you note after an interview is a common practice that can strengthen your candidacy and leave a positive impression on the interviewer. It shows appreciation for the opportunity to interview, reiterates your interest in the position, and allows you to express key points you may have missed during the interview.

Why Send a Thank-You Note?

- Express Gratitude: A thank-you note is a polite way to acknowledge the interviewer's time and effort in considering you for the position.

- Reiterate Interest: It provides a platform for you to reemphasize your interest in the role and the company.

- Stay Top of Mind: Sending a thank-you note keeps you fresh in the interviewer's memory, especially if they are seeing many candidates.

Tips for Writing an Effective Thank-You Note:

- Timeliness: Send the thank-you note within 24 hours of the interview to make a timely impression.

- Personalization: Reference specific points of the interview or topics discussed to make it personalized.

- Professionalism: Use a professional tone and language, avoiding casual or overly familiar language.

- Clarity: Be clear and concise in your message, focusing on key points you want to convey.

- Proofread: Always proofread your thank-you note to ensure there are no spelling or grammatical errors.

Example of a Thank-You Note:

Dear [Interviewer's Name],

I wanted to take a moment to express my gratitude for the opportunity to interview with you and the [Company Name] team yesterday. I thoroughly enjoyed our discussion about [specific topic] and was impressed by the company's commitment to [mention a company value or initiative].

Our conversation further solidified my enthusiasm for the [Job Title] position, and I am excited about the prospect of contributing to [Company Name]. I am particularly drawn to [mention a specific aspect of the role or company] and believe that my skills and experience align well with the requirements of the role.

Thank you once again for considering my application. I look forward to the possibility of contributing to the innovative work being done at [Company Name]. Please feel free to reach out if you need any further information from me.

Warm regards,
  [Your Name]

2. Strategies for Post-Interview Communication

Beyond sending a thank-you note, there are additional strategies for post-interview communication that can help you stand out as a strong candidate. These strategies include following up on timelines, asking for feedback, and maintaining a positive and professional demeanor throughout the process.

Key Strategies for Post-Interview Communication:

- Follow-Up on Promised Timelines: If the interviewer mentioned a specific timeline for a decision, it is appropriate to follow up after that time has passed if you have not heard back. This shows your continued interest in the position.

- Request Feedback: If you receive a rejection or have not heard back after a follow-up, consider requesting feedback on your interview performance. This can provide valuable insights for future interviews.

- Stay Polite and Professional: Regardless of the outcome of the interview, maintain a positive and professional attitude in all communications with the employer. This demonstrates maturity and professionalism.

- Customize Your Approach: Tailor your post-interview communications based on the specifics of the interview and the company culture. A one-size-fits-all approach may not be as effective.

- Use Multiple Channels: In addition to email, consider reaching out through LinkedIn or other professional networking platforms to stay connected with the interviewer and showcase your continued interest.

Example of Post-Interview Follow-Up Email:

Subject: Follow-Up on Interview for [Job Title] Position

Dear [Interviewer's Name],

I hope this message finds you well. I wanted to follow up regarding the interview we had for the [Job Title] position on [Interview Date]. I understand that your team is likely in the process of making a decision, and I wanted to reiterate my interest and enthusiasm for the role.

I am very excited about the possibility of contributing to the innovative projects at [Company Name] and believe that my skills and experiences align well with the requirements of the position. I am looking forward to the opportunity to bring my expertise to the team and help drive [specific goal or project mentioned during the interview].

If there are any additional details or information that you require from me, please do not hesitate to reach out. I appreciate the time and consideration you have given to my application and look forward to the possibility of working together.

Thank you for your time and consideration.

Warm regards,
  [Your Name]

Conclusion

Follow-up is an essential component of the job search process, particularly after an interview. Sending a thank-you note and employing effective strategies for post-interview communication can significantly impact your candidacy and set you apart from other applicants. By expressing gratitude, reiterating interest, and maintaining professionalism in your communications, you can leave a positive impression on potential employers and increase your chances of securing the job. Remember to tailor your approach to each interview and company to make a lasting impact.

13

Dealing with Rejection

Dealing with rejection is a common aspect of life that many people face at some point. It can come in various forms such as job rejections, romantic rejections, project rejections, or any situation where you do not get the response you hoped for. How individuals cope with rejection and use the feedback provided as a tool for improvement can greatly impact their personal and professional growth.

Coping with Rejection

1. Accepting Emotions: It's important to acknowledge and accept your emotions when faced with rejection. It's normal to feel hurt, disappointed, or even angry. Suppressing these emotions can be harmful in the long run. Recognizing and allowing yourself to feel these emotions is the first step in coping with rejection.

2. Self-Compassion: Treat yourself with kindness and understanding. Rejection does not define your worth as a person.

Practice self-compassion by reminding yourself that everyone faces rejection at some point in their lives.

3. Perspective: Try to gain perspective on the situation. Rejection is often not a reflection of your abilities or worth but might be due to external factors or circumstances. Understanding this can help you move forward with a positive mindset.

4. Seek Support: Talk to friends, family, or a therapist about your feelings of rejection. Sharing your experiences with someone you trust can provide a sense of relief and help you gain new insights into the situation.

5. Focus on Growth: Use rejection as an opportunity for personal growth. Reflect on what you can learn from the experience and how you can improve in the future. Every rejection can be a stepping stone towards success if you approach it with a growth mindset.

6. Maintain a Routine: Continuing with your daily routine can provide a sense of normalcy and stability during times of rejection. Engage in activities that bring you joy and fulfillment to counteract negative feelings.

7. Setbacks vs. Failures: Differentiate between setbacks and failures. Setbacks are temporary obstacles that can be overcome with effort and perseverance. Viewing rejection as a setback rather than a failure can help you stay motivated and focused on your goals.

8. Rejection as a Learning Experience: Embrace rejection as a

learning experience. Analyze the feedback provided, identify areas for improvement, and use this knowledge to enhance your skills and performance in the future.

Using Feedback for Improvement

Feedback, especially in the context of rejection, can be a valuable source of information that offers insights into areas where you can grow and develop. Here are some ways you can leverage feedback for improvement:

1. Openness to Feedback: Cultivate a mindset that is open to receiving feedback, whether positive or negative. Constructive criticism can provide valuable insights that you may not have been aware of.

2. Analyzing Feedback: Take the time to analyze the feedback you receive. What are the specific points mentioned? Are there recurring themes or patterns in the feedback? Understanding the feedback in detail can help you identify areas for improvement.

3. Actionable Steps: Translate the feedback into actionable steps. Break down the feedback into specific actions you can take to address the areas highlighted. This could involve acquiring new skills, changing behaviors, or adjusting your approach.

4. Seek Clarifications: If the feedback received is unclear or vague, don't hesitate to seek clarification. Ask for specific examples or instances that can help you better understand the feedback and how to implement changes.

5. Create a Development Plan: Develop a plan based on the feedback you've received. Set clear goals and timelines for implementing changes and track your progress over time. Having a structured plan can help you stay focused and committed to improvement.

6. Practice and Feedback Loop: Practice the new skills or behaviors you're working on and seek feedback on your progress. Regular feedback loops can help you gauge your improvement and make necessary adjustments along the way.

7. Celebrate Progress: Acknowledge and celebrate the progress you make based on the feedback received. Recognizing your growth and development can boost your confidence and motivation to continue improving.

8. Continuous Improvement: View feedback as a continuous process of growth and improvement. Embrace a mindset that is constantly seeking opportunities for learning and development, both from feedback received and your own reflections.

Example Scenarios:

Coping with Rejection

Scenario 1: Job Rejection

Situation: You applied for a job you were excited about and went through multiple rounds of interviews. However, you receive an email informing you that another candidate was selected for the position.

Coping Strategies:

- Accepting Emotions: Allow yourself to feel disappointed but remind yourself that rejection is part of the job search process.
- Seek Support: Reach out to a mentor or career counselor to discuss your job search strategy and how you can improve.
- Focus on Growth: Identify areas where you can enhance your skills or experience to increase your chances of success in future job applications.

Scenario 2: Romantic Rejection

Situation: You express your feelings to someone you have feelings for, but they do not reciprocate and see you only as a friend.

Coping Strategies:

- Self-Compassion: Be kind to yourself and acknowledge that romantic feelings are not always mutual.
- Perspective: Understand that compatibility is essential in relationships and that this rejection may lead you to find someone who is a better match.
- Maintain a Routine: Continue engaging in activities that bring you joy and fulfillment to help you move forward.

Using Feedback for Improvement

Scenario 1: Project Rejection

Situation: Your project proposal was rejected by the review

committee for lack of clarity and feasibility.

Feedback:

- The proposal lacked a clear timeline for project milestones.
    - The budget allocation was not justified adequately.
    - The proposed methodology was deemed too ambitious for the resources available.

Actionable Steps:

- Develop a Detailed Timeline: Revise the proposal to include a clear timeline with specific milestones and deadlines.
    - Budget Justification: Provide detailed explanations for each budget item and how it contributes to the project's success.
    - Reevaluate Methodology: Simplify the methodology to align with the available resources and demonstrate feasibility.

Scenario 2: Performance Review Feedback

Situation: During your annual performance review, your supervisor provides feedback on areas where you need improvement.

Feedback:

- Communication skills need improvement, especially in team settings.
    - Time management could be more efficient to meet project deadlines.
    - Develop a stronger presence during client presentations.

Development Plan:

- Communication Skills: Enroll in a communication skills workshop to enhance your ability to convey ideas clearly and effectively.
- Time Management: Implement a time management system to prioritize tasks and allocate time efficiently.
- Presentation Skills: Practice client presentations and seek feedback from colleagues to improve your presence and delivery.

In conclusion, dealing with rejection and using feedback for improvement are essential skills that can foster personal and professional growth. By approaching rejection with resilience, self-compassion, and a growth mindset, individuals can turn setbacks into opportunities for learning and development. Feedback, whether positive or negative, serves as a valuable tool for identifying areas of improvement and taking proactive steps towards reaching one's full potential. Embracing rejection as a natural part of life's journey and leveraging feedback for continuous growth can lead to greater self-awareness, skill enhancement, and ultimately, success in various aspects of life.

www.ingramcontent.com/pod-product-compliance
Lightning Source LLC
Chambersburg PA
CBHW050118230526
45470CB00004B/1884